Monastic Life

A Sign of Contradiction to the Fashionable Idols

Bonnie B. Thurston

SLG Press
Convent of the Incarnation
Fairacres Parker Street
Oxford England
www.slgpress.co.uk

First published by SLG Press 2016

ISBN: 978-0-7283-0252-5 (Paper)
ISBN: 978-0-7283-0281-5 (ePub)
ISBN: 978-0-7283-0282-2 (MOBI)

Cover Picture: The Lamb of God, central roof boss, ceiling of the Chapter House, York Minster.

Printed by Parchments of Oxford
www.parchmentuk.com

Monastic Life

A Sign of Contradiction to the
Fashionable Idols

Preface

The text of this work was originally presented as two lectures at the Monastic Institute at St. John's Abbey and School of Theology in Collegeville, MN in June 2014. The theme of the Institute was 'Imagining the Future: Monastic Life in 2020.' I am grateful to have had the opportunity to share in the Institute and for the very kind hospitality I received at St. John's.

Several quotations in this essay were penned long before inclusive language was the norm for serious discourse. I am sure they will grate on some ears, but I am, in part, a scholar and not willing to alter original materials. If an apology is required, this is it.

Bonnie B. Thurston
West Virginia. USA
November 2015

CONTENTS

Introduction

Let me begin with my basic assumption about monastic life. It is that there is a magnetism in God that it is impossible for some people to resist. Those divine energies of which Gregory Palamas wrote are not only irresistible, but, to use Paul Tillich's phrase, of 'ultimate concern' to some. *How* we are drawn, *how* we respond to God's magnetism varies with our social circumstances, our natural gifts, our family's religious tradition (if it had one); any number of external things. But *that* we are irresistibly drawn by the Love that created, redeemed and sustains us, and everything that exists, is the basic reality of our lives.

As I see it, the function of monasticism as an institution within an institution is to praise God and to protect the charism of those called to such a life to make it possible to clear away as much distraction as possible. Such a person can spend his or her time and energy in the search for God putting one's self in a place where God can find one—not talking about God or theorizing about God, but actually attending to God. As Jean Leclercq said in *The Love of Learning and the Desire for God* (a book from which I shall quote several times), it is 'to seek God and not to discuss Him …'[1] Leclercq continues:

> All else, including intellectual pursuits, should remain subordinate to the search for God. Nothing should interfere with the monk's living in

---

[1] Jean Leclercq OSB, *The Love of Learning and the Desire for God* (Catharine Misrahi, translator (NY: Fordham U. Press, 1961/77) 254.

the presence of God, that is to say, with humility
as St Benedict conceives it.'[2]

'Living in the presence of God' is an interesting definition of humility.

Two biblical images come to mind: Egypt and Babel. The person inexorably drawn to God leaves Egypt, not because Egypt is corrupt — which, by and large it is, those pyramids being the symbol of ego out of control — but because the wilderness of Sinai is the locus of liberation. It is the place where a person finds freedom because she or he is completely dependent upon God both psychologically and physically. The person drawn to God flees Babel (its tower the classic biblical image of *hubris*) because there is something, indeed, Someone, to be found only in an authentic leisure, freedom from the making of bricks, and a silence into which an authentic word can be dropped. A wisp of divine music waits to be heard. We need to put ourselves where we can hear it. As André Louf wrote in *The Cistercian Way*, 'The monastic life has no other objective than to awaken the heart and make it aware of the prayer which is always going on within us.'[3]

I think Philippians 2: 1–5, the introduction to the Christ Hymn (2: 6–11), which may be the oldest material in the New Testament, contains the monastic project in miniature:

> If then there is any encouragement in Christ, any consolation from love, any sharing in the Spirit, any compassion and sympathy, make my joy complete: be of the same mind, having the same

---

[2] Ibid.

[3] Andre Louf, *The Cistercian Way* (Kalamazoo, Cistercian Publications, 1989) 74.

love, being in full accord and of one mind. Do nothing from selfish ambition or conceit, but in humility regard others as better than yourselves. Let each of you look not to your own interests, but to the interests of others. Let the same mind be in you that was in Christ Jesus …

The first four verses are a single sentence in Greek, a series of conditional clauses premised on the opening construction, the 'if' clause, which assumes the affirmative response. There *is* 'consolation in love,' 'sharing in the Spirit,' 'compassion,' and 'sympathy' (or 'tenderness'). Forms of 'one' and of *phroneo*, meaning holding an opinion, being of an attitude, 'minded' or 'disposed', dominate the sentence. So a community of 'one-mindedness' arises of people who are not selfishly ambitious or conceited, but humble, attending to the interests of others, and Christ-minded. The virtues Paul advances here are the great virtues of Christian monasticism.

My root assumption about monasticism is twofold: first, that God, for probably mysterious reasons because the persons are often unlikely, draws some people so strongly that God alone becomes their primary concern; and, second, that monasteries should be places where precisely those people can flourish. Monasteries are places for the contemplative's vision and the prophet's voice.

Professor Patrick O'Connell of Gannon University in Erie, Pennsylvania, is doing a great service by editing Thomas Merton's unpublished talks, given largely during the time Merton was Master of Scholastics and of Novices at Our Lady of Gethsemani Abbey in Kentucky.

Cistercian Publications/Liturgical Press is publishing those volumes in the Monastic Wisdom series. I had the privilege of reviewing *The Life of the Vows.* A note in O'Connell's introduction gave me the idea for this reflection. Writing about Merton on *conversatio morum,* O'Connell notes:

> … a superficial embrace of what passes for the latest wisdom risks distorting or trivializing the genuinely contemplative and prophetic role of monasticism to serve as a sign of contradiction to all easy accommodation, in any era, to the fashionable idols of the age.[4]

In what follows, I share some thoughts about the contemplative (the identity) and the prophetic (the mission) as they seem to me essential to monasticism, the terrain of monastic observance if you will.

The contemplative's vision and the prophet's voice are two sides of the monastic coin. The contemplative vision arises from a conviction that—or the experience of—a perhaps unseen Reality is worth giving one's whole life to. The contemplative lives toward and in that Reality. The prophet's 'voice' might be a misnomer, since sound is secondary to it. Remember St Francis of Assisi: 'Preach the gospel at all times. Use words if necessary.' Or St Vincent de Paul: 'If God is the centre of your life, no words are necessary. Your mere presence will touch hearts.' The prophet's 'voice,' is seen as much as heard, seen precisely in the monastic's life of *conversatio morum,* that radical alternative that inevitably challenges the status quo (and normally scares the dickens out of those

---

[4]Patrick O'Connell (ed.), *Thomas Merton: The Life of the Vows* (Monastic Wisdom Series 30) (Collegeville, MN: Liturgical Press, 2012) lxii–lxiii).

embroiled in it). So the monastic presence in society is far from 'mere.' I have an inkling its sign of contradiction to our business-as-usual society is likely to be salvific for everyone.

In the first section of this monograph we will explore 'The Contemplative's Vision'. In the second, we will think about the 'The Prophet's Voice'. Both are contradictory, that is, against the speech, or taking issue with, pointing up the incongruities of, unexamined life in society. (By the way, another of my basic assumptions is that the way things are is not only not the way things have to be, but probably are not what God intended.) I hope this material will give you some ingredients from which you can make a meal. I am not worried about the future of monasticism because that which pleases God endures. Certainly it must please God to be sought. And, as God is the Great Seeker of us, to seek God is to mirror one of God's own fundamental attributes.

The Contemplative's Vision

I go through periods of time when I think that if I hear the word 'contemplative' one more time, I'll not only growl, but bite someone on the ankle. Hard. Contemplation is an indefinable term because it is an inanimate attitude, one of those things you cannot define (and therefore probably cannot teach), but you know it when you see it, and you can catch it from somebody who has it. When it comes to putting words to it, nobody I know about has much improved on the first chapter of Thomas Merton's classic *New Seeds of Contemplation*. Let me remind you of a few things he says in that chapter entitled, 'What Is Contemplation?'

> Contemplation is the highest expression of … intellectual and spiritual life. It is that life … fully awake, fully active, fully aware that it is alive. It is spiritual wonder. It is spontaneous awe at the sacredness of life, of being. It is gratitude for life, for awareness and for being. It is a vivid realization of the fact that life and being in us proceed from an invisible, transcendent and infinitely abundant Source. Contemplation is … awareness of the reality of that Source. It *knows* the Source … with a certitude that goes beyond both reason and simple faith.[1]

> … contemplation is a sudden gift of awareness, an awakening to the Real within all that is real. A vivid awareness of infinite Being at the roots of our own limited being. An awareness of our

---

[1]Thomas Merton, *New Seeds of Contemplation* (NY: New Directions, 1961/72) 1 (Merton's italics).

contingent reality as received, as a present from God, as a free gift of love.[2]

Merton points out that contemplation is a gift that reflects the Source of Reality, of Being itself, a gift given in love. So the question arises, 'How would you see this gift manifest in a person or in a religious community?' Or, put another way, 'What characterizes the contemplative?' I suggest four qualities: holy leisure, refusal of distraction, detachment, and life at a human pace.

Holy Leisure

Jean Leclercq said that everything should be subordinate to the search for God. That principle is the root of holy leisure. It does not mean we should not work for our bread. (Parenthetically, I am convinced that if the heads of multinational corporations and the boards of directors of big companies had actually to do work with their hands our economic messes would straighten out rather quickly.) It is not only perfectly appropriate, but spiritually a good thing to earn our living by making cheese or fudge or jam or fruitcake, or by printing or selling books and cards, or by welcoming pilgrim guests. In fact, work makes us close to St Joseph, the patron saint of workers, and to the 'little ones' whom Matthew's Jesus says God specially cares for. Work draws us close to Jesus the *tekton*, the skilled craftsman, a better translation of the Greek than the traditional 'carpenter'.

The work of our hands is intrinsically related to the vow of poverty. Benedict commands work in his Rule (RB 48), and Cassian said that work is the anchor that

---

[2]Ibid. 3.

stabilizes the boat of our heart.[3] What is not OK is to live for the sake of work and not work in order to live the life. Like so many things, work is a good servant and a dreadful master. When cheese, or jam, or cards, or guests are more important than the Office, or individual meditation, or time to potter about in the cloister garden in the cool of the evening, something has gone seriously wrong. Undoubtedly knowing the idealism of his statement, Leclercq wrote 'The whole organization of monastic life is dominated by the solicitude for safeguarding a certain spiritual leisure, a certain freedom in the interest of prayer in all its forms and, above all, authentic contemplative peace.'[4]

What I am talking about is what classic monastic texts call *otium*, life in the 'cloistered paradise' which is described with words like *otium, quies, vacatio, sabbatum*. *Otium* might be translated 'free time' by the cynical and 'ease' by the saint. It lives somewhere between the extremes of obsessive overwork and sloth. It balances prayer and work. Leclercq says, '*Otium* is the major occupation of the monk.'[5] Dom Andre Louf devotes a chapter in his book on the Cistercian Life to it. Chapter 8 is tellingly entitled 'Laborious Leisure' and states '… the leisure of monastic life should be entirely occupied with the inner activity of the heart.'[6] The contemplative vision is clear when one works whole-heartedly for the sake of everybody's whole heart.

---

[3] Quoted in Louf, 115.
[4] Leclercq, 24.
[5] Leclercq, 84.
[6] Louf, 114.

This leads directly to the second observable quality of the contemplative vision, refusal of distraction. One of the greatest allies of The Enemy has always been distraction. Who knew that technology companies that make electronic gizmos and the software that runs them are now working for him? Almost any serious monastic writing contains warnings about distraction. Cassian, for example, speaks of *ataraxia*. It is a very strong Greek word. In Greek, if you want to negate the meaning of a word, you put an alpha, an 'a', in front of it. This is called an 'alpha privative', and the new word means NOT whatever the substantive was. *Tarasso* is a Greek verb that means 'trouble, disturb, upset, terrify, stir up'. So *ataraxia* means not troubled, not disturbed, at peace in one's soul.[7]

Imagine my surprise to find a whole article on this in an unlikely theological source, *The New Yorker* magazine. The article 'Only Disconnect, Two Cheers for Boredom' ran in the issue of 28 October 2013. In it, Evgeny Morozov wrote about the ubiquity of distractions in modern life, which he thinks are coping mechanisms that blunt our ability to react to life, and thus are opposed to Merton's sense that the contemplative is fully awake, alive and aware. Morozov writes 'these days, "the state of permanent receptivity" has become the birthright of anyone with a smartphone. We are under constant assault by "interestingness"...'[8] Later in the essay (which reviews three serious recent books on the problem of

---

[7] I first encountered the word in Owen Chadwick's excellent study *John Cassian* (2nd ed.) (Cambridge: Cambridge U. Press, 1968) 83.

[8] Evgeny Morozov, 'Only Disconnect', *The New Yorker* (28 October 2013) 33.

distraction, one tellingly entitled *The Distraction Addiction*), he calls distraction 'sensory overload'. He quotes a Dutch media scholar, Christoph Lindner, who says that 'smart cities ought to create "slow-spots" — pockets of silence and attention that could house "creative sites of decelerated practice and experience".'[9] Does that sound at all familiar? Perhaps before long monasteries will be the only such 'slow spots'. Many of them certainly currently provide that space now.

In one of those peculiar and frequent synchronicities we notice when we aren't distracted, the day I was writing this, the May 2014 edition of the Buddhist magazine *Shambhala Sun* arrived. 'The real problem with Distraction: it keeps you from enlightenment' was emblazoned on the cover of an edition devoted to the dangers of distraction. At an earlier period of my life, I was deeply engaged with Buddhist-Christian dialogue. Although I admire the precision of their analysis of spiritual psychology, I'm not a Buddhist; but it worries me that the people who come to me for spiritual companionship, who own the most advanced and distracting gadgets, are people in leadership in their religious communities. Anecdotal evidence, to be sure, but it demonstrates the extent to which society embraces distraction.

The contemplative vision encourages serious examination of the distractions that are part of the fashionable idols of this, or any age. All those communication devices—from the old transistor radios and TVs of my youth to laptops, tablets and smart-phones—are two-edged swords. They may be like work,

---

[9] Ibid. 36–37.

useful if done with the proper attitude. The problem is that they can blunt that proper attitude, and all the little demons stomp and cheer and pump the air with their tiny fists as they do so. The static God has to penetrate to reach us is, as it always has been, of our own making. But these days a lot of it could be unplugged and powered off *if* the dangers of technology are recognized. One of the most serious dangers of distractions is that they keep us from being present where we are, and not being present is inevitably a kind of spiritual suicide. For more on this point I refer you to David Steindl-Rast's work, especially *A Listening Heart*,[10] and to Richard Rohr's *The Naked Now*[11].

Just as an aside, I think that one of the great gifts of the Buddhist tradition is precisely its focus on the present moment as the locus of spiritual experience and wisdom. Thomas Merton's poem 'Song: If You Seek...' calls the present moment

> The 'now' that cuts
> Time like a blade.
>
> ... the unexpected flash
> Beyond 'yes,' beyond 'no,'
> The forerunner of the Word of God.[12]

Detachment

I recognize the ubiquity of the multiple modes of distraction, and realize that refusal of them would mean that monastic life would exhibit detachment from the way the world is. Good. My premise is that monasteries exist to

---

[10] David Steindl-Rast, OSB, *A Listening Heart* (NY: Crossroad, 1983/1999).

[11] Richard Rohr, *The Naked Now* (NY: Crossroad Publishing, 2009).

[12] Thomas Merton, *The Collected Poems of Thomas Merton* (NY: New Directions, 1977) 340.

support those who, like Jesus *driven* into the wilderness, *have* to leave the world in order to pursue and be found by the God. In the deathless words of Francis Thompson's poem 'The Hound of Heaven', this is the God whose '… strong Feet … followed, followed after. / But with unhurrying chase, And unperturbed pace.'

A good novitiate allows the novice to bring in and grow his or her passion for God while gently detaching from all that distracts from that growth. The tricky bit is that the dangerous distractions will be different for each novice. What is benign for one might destroy another. Monastic formation is about detachment from one set of things for attachment to another. This is another reason why serious discernment is necessary to determine how much of 'the world' can be allowed to take up residence in the monastery.

Detachment from one's own preferences about how to dress, what to eat, how to distract oneself, what books one may read, or when one may shower and with whose choice of shampoo, important as they are for monastic formation, don't really touch the deeper value of detachment in the spiritual life. The more embroiled we are in the local and personally systemic, the less easy it is for us to see the big picture. For example, as my contemporaries have become grandparents (a wonderful thing, to be sure) their worlds have correspondingly contracted. A professor friend who planned to spend retirement teaching in Africa now hopes to live near grandchildren. Folks who have spent their lives — and I do mean *spent*, as in given, poured out, expended — in a single business or one school or parish or one ministry sometimes allow those institutions to delimit the size of their world.

Put another way, there are things you can see from the sidelines that you miss if you are playing in the game. I think God needs a few folks on the sidelines who can really see what is going on and speak the prophetic word to the players and the teams. Since that word is often something like, 'the king is naked!' it is not surprising that, in one way or another, such persons are silenced. Marginality is spiritually both crucially important and usually very dangerous personally.

Benedict suggests that we must 'become detached from all immediate interests, devoting [ourselves] in silence and in withdrawal from the world to prayer and asceticism'. 'According to St Benedict, monastic life is entirely disinterested.'[13] Benedict does not say 'dispassionate'. He does not mean that we do not care about the world's suffering. In fact, our detachment from it can help us recognize its real evils. It is not surprising that women religious in the USA were among the first to recognize human trafficking and to organize themselves against it. Benedict does mean that we not be so embroiled in, so focused on, our little corner of God's world (perhaps also seeking power or influence or authority there), that we lose the big picture and thus the ability to speak the prophetic word. Merton said contemplation is life fully awake and fully aware. The image of detachment is not that of the ostrich with its head in the sand, but of the owl watching with wisdom from the encircling trees.

The most difficult detachment is from the results of our own efforts. In *Conjectures of a Guilty Bystander* Merton wrote, 'Detachment is not pure indifference, but … concentration of attention on the subject of the act

---

[13] Quoted in Leclercq, 24.

itself, not on the results or the consequences.'[14] On this point Merton's letter of 21 February 1966 to Jim Forest, then leader of the Catholic Peace Fellowship, is an important, although neglected, teaching. He suggests that all we

> can ever hope for in terms of visible results is that we will have perhaps contributed *something* to a clarification of Christian truth in this society, and as a result a *few* people may have … opened up to the Grace of God and made some sense out of their lives. The real hope … is not in something we think we can do, but in God who is making something good out of it in some way we cannot see.[15]

This is as true of monasticism as of any other effort.

We live in a world of people desperately over-scheduled and sinfully busy. I think people often fill their lives with distractions precisely to avoid the big quest-ions. Some people over-schedule themselves, especially with good works, to convince themselves that they are important, that their lives have meaning. Misuse of time by over-scheduling is the modern equivalent of Adam and Eve hiding in the bushes when God wants to spend an evening with them. I have observed that the busier a person is, the more distracted he or she tends to be. It is why cell phones launch those nasty little jingles in the midst of liturgy. Some folks cannot even turn them off for God. Bernard suggests 'the criterion of the true mystic …

---

[14] Thomas Merton, *Conjectures of a Guilty Bystander* (NY: Doubleday/ Image, 1968) 120.

[15] William H. Shannon (ed.), Thomas Merton: *The Hidden Ground of Love: Letters* (NY: Farrar, Straus, Giroux, 1985) 296 & 297. Italics in the original.

is … detachment'.[16] Another criterion is certainly that the mystic lives at a human pace.

Human Pace

Another way to talk about detachment is to remind ourselves that God apparently planned creation to move at the pace of 'holy leisure'. Human beings are supposed to live at a human pace, not at the speed of light or of a gazillion gigabytes a second. Some years ago, I learned this the hard way, and wrote a small book about that hard won knowledge.[17] I would have been wise to pay more attention to the amount of space Benedict devotes in his Rule to the organization of time in the monastery. So here is the fifty-dollar question: Why would anyone want to go to a residential institution where life is as harried as it is in mainstream society?

Interestingly, the financial column in the 27 January 2014 *New Yorker* (back to that source of spiritual wisdom!) was entitled 'The Cult of Overwork'. It reported how big firms like Bank of America and Credit Suisse no longer require young financial analysts to work fifteen hours a day and on Saturdays, foregoing, as the author James Surowiecki put it, 'anything resembling a normal life'. It was quite a frightening article because it gave the statistics for what we have suspected all along. The author noted, 'The perplexing thing about the cult of overwork is that, as we've known for a while, long hours diminish both productivity and quality'. He concludes, 'In a culture that venerates overwork, people internalize

---

[16] Leclercq, 319.

[17] Bonnie Thurston, *To Everything a Season: A Spirituality of Time* (NY: Crossroad, 1999) (Eugene, OR: Wipf and Stock, 1999/2004).

crazy hours as the norm'.[18] The religious lexical field of the article, which used words like 'cult' and 'venerate', was not lost on me. Nor was the reality that the cult of overwork thwarts the contemplative vision.

I have known monastics, good monastics, whose time choices suggested that they felt they were not good community members if they were not working every minute they were not in choir. I wonder if this sets a good example for novices. In small communities especially, there is a lot of necessary work and not many hands to do it; that does not give such a community licence for the kind of overwork which leads to a certain frenzy and 'tempest in teapot' episodes. Living at a human pace of the sort Benedict envisioned, with a balanced life of adequate rest and sensible work hours, both of which are for the sake of prayer, means living a life of 'holy leisure'. Such a life might be the one in which Francis Thompson's God 'with unhurrying chase, And unperturbed pace' might most easily find one. If anyone in the universe has a lot of work to do, it is God, and all of us in our lives of prayer have at one time or another noted the leisurely pace at which God does it!

Keeping Sabbath is about knowing when to stop. Most of us would never dream of 'bearing false witness', 'doing murder', 'committing adultery', but we blithely break the *commandment* to keep Sabbath. God worked six days, and then God stopped. God had made enough stuff. I think God's knowing when to quit is a mark of divinity. Perhaps our knowing when to stop and to rest might be—is—as well, a mark of our 'divinization', as the Eastern Church calls it.

---

[18] James Surowiecki, 'The Cult of Overwork', (The Financial Page) *The New Yorker* (27 January 2014) 23.

You do not have to read far in Merton's monastic journals to encounter his whingeing about the monastery's attitude toward work. I do not know whether he was accurate, but I do think his analysis of overwork is spiritually spot-on. He writes in *Conjectures of a Guilty Bystander*:

> ... there is a pervasive form of contemporary violence to which the idealist ... most easily succumbs: activism and overwork. The rush and pressure of modern life are a form, perhaps the most common form, of its innate violence. To allow oneself to be carried away by a multitude of conflicting concerns, to surrender to too many demands, to commit oneself to too many projects ... is to succumb to violence. ... it is cooperation in violence.[19]

Overwork is an insidious form of violence which Merton thinks destroys not only our inner peace, but the root of our inner wisdom. Here is the very best quotation I know about monastic life at a human pace. It is from an essay on Benedictine Spirituality by Jacques Winandy, then Abbot of Clairvaux: 'To reform a monastery is to restore its rest.'[20]

Conclusion

The contemplative vision that I hope monasticism never loses will always manifest four qualities: holy leisure,

---

[19] Thomas Merton, *Conjectures of a Guilty Bystander* (NY: Doubleday, 1966) 73.

[20] Jacques Winandy, 'Benedictine Spirituality', 28. This is a chapter from a book section called 'Some Schools of Spirituality'. I was sent the chapter without any bibliographical information and regret that I am unable to provide it.

refusal of distraction, detachment, and a human pace. I hope my reflections have made their relationship to one another clear, for they are in fact almost inseparable. Ideally all four will be enveloped in a delicious sense of humour without which any form of life is insipid, which as Latin scholars know, means 'without salt', 'tasteless', without the saltiness that Jesus commands his disciples to exhibit. It was in part a sense of humour in the context of a highly regulated life that first drew me to monasticism and has kept me close to it for nearly forty years.

On the 18 March 1978, during my first ever residence at a monastery, I turned a corner in the convent of All Saints Sisters of the Poor, near Catonsville, Maryland. I entered a corridor of a kind that exists in many religious houses: that long hall with windows along the length on one side, and light reflecting off the bare, white walls and beautifully polished wooden floor. A sister (in full habit, of course) was meticulously sweeping the already spotless floor with a push broom while the community watchdog, a miniature French poodle, repeatedly attacked the broom with tiny, ferocious growls. The sister, who had not seen me, beamed with the silliness of it and participated in the game; she was clearly struggling not to laugh aloud because it was still the Great Silence. In the midst of doing the daily task and keeping the Rule, the sheer joy and delight of life bubbled forth so clearly that even an over-awed first-time guest and harried graduate student got—and never for-got—its message.

The busy-ness, overwork, distractedness and grasping that characterize much of modern life are often evasions of the big questions. Perhaps the biggest is an ancient, traditional monastic query: *ad quid venisti*? What have you come here to do? As Paul Tillich would put it,

'What is your ultimate concern?' or, 'To what would you sacrifice all else?' Now, and in the future, monastic life might be best organized around such a central principle, Teilhard's omega point, if you will. As you now know, my own view is that monasteries exist to praise God and to protect the charism of those who seek God alone.

But, as I confessed at the outset, I am not a monastic, so you must both pose and answer your own big questions, bearing in mind that the questions are probably more important than the answers, in part because the question asked determines the answer one gets. Let me offer you an image: that of a prism refracting multiple rays of light. Perhaps a fruitful question for you might be 'What is the point through which all the bands of colour in our community are refracted into fire?'

Transition:
The Meaning of 'Prophet'

WE have considered monasticism's contemplative identity. Now I want to consider the other side of the monastic coin, its prophetic voice, its mission. Bear in mind that its most potent voice is not in words, as St Francis of Assisi and St Vincent de Paul have pointed out, but in the life itself, especially as it is manifested in consistency and in its counter-cultural ways of proceeding. We are still in the realm of *conversatio morum*. Patrick O'Connell observes, in his introduction to Merton's *The Life of the Vows*, that

> … a superficial embrace of what passes for the latest wisdom risks distorting or trivializing the genuinely contemplative and prophetic role of monasticism to serve as a sign of contradiction to all easy accommodation, in any era, to the fashionable idols of the age.[1]

A quotation at the beginning of Jean Leclercq's *The Love of Learning and the Desire for God* makes an important connection between the contemplative and the prophetic. He writes:

> In a secular usage, *meditari* means, in a general way, to think, to reflect; … but more than these, it often implies an affinity with the practical or even moral order. It implies thinking of a thing with the intent to do it … to prepare oneself for it, to

---

[1] Patrick F. O'Connell (ed.), *Thomas Merton: The Life of the Vows* (Monastic Wisdom Series 30), (Collegeville, MN: Liturgical Press, 2012) lxii–lxiii.

21

prefigure it in the mind, to desire it, in a way, to do it in advance, briefly, to practice it.[2]

In monasticism, the inner life prepares one for and, indeed, propels one into, the practical, moral life. I think it is not overstating the case to say that the contemplative prepares us for, sustains us in, and requires of us the prophetic.

What do we mean by the prophetic? The biblical word 'prophet' is a Greek compound formed of the preposition *pro* (for) and the verb *phami* (to speak). The prophet is one who speaks for God, who sees the world from God's perspective or through God's eyes. In *The Prophets: An Introduction*, Rabbi Abraham Heschel teaches that 'the prophet is an iconoclast, challenging the apparently holy, revered, and awesome.'[3] Heschel suggests that 'the purpose of prophecy is to conquer callousness, to change the inner man as well as to revolutionize history.'[4] Obviously, this is not a comfortable assignment. Perhaps we can compare the prophet's role to the priestly role of the *pontus*, the bridge between people and God. The prophet 'stands between' with the purpose of uniting God and the people of his or her community. Heschel says the prophet's 'true greatness is [the] ability to hold God and man in a single thought', and his or her main task 'is to bring the world into divine focus'[5]. The prophet expresses what Heschel calls 'divine pathos', the feelings of God. In his chapter on

---

[2] Jean Leclercq OSB, *The Love of Learning and the Desire for God* (NY: Fordham University Press, 1961/1974) 20.

[3] Abraham J. Heschel, *The Prophets: An Introduction* (NY: Harper Torch Books, 1969) 10.

[4] Ibid. 17.

[5] Ibid. 21, 24.

Jeremiah, the section about God's sorrow and broken-heartedness, necessarily shared by the prophet, is a profoundly moving insight into God's nature. Heschel helps us see the connections between the prophetic and the monastic. If you do not yet know his work, it is well worth investigating further. You might find it, as I did, a life-changing experience.

It is important to note that prophets speak 'against' because prophets love. Biblical prophets railed against Israel's institutions precisely because they loved them, and the community formed around them. Prophets rail for the same that reason parents sometimes rail, because they love those entrusted to them. One of the best essays that I know on the reason for monastic life, Thomas Merton's brilliant introductory essay to *The Wisdom of the Desert,* reminds us that our ancient ancestors did not flee the world because they hated it, but because they loved it, and by their detachment hoped to save it.[6]

In the biblical tradition, prophecy assumes something is amiss. The prophet's voice is both contra and pro: *against* the fashionable idols, and *for* God's loving plan for human community. Accommodation to all kinds of idols has always been easy because they are normally enshrined as 'the way things are', the accepted wisdom of a society, implied when what 'they' say is quoted, without any idea of who 'they' might be. The fashionable idols are usually on display in the status quo, and throughout human history they have remained essentially unchanged. They are power, money, and sex, often worshipped in their avatars, self-assertion and prestige. These idols are always and everywhere in

---

[6] Thomas Merton, *The Wisdom of the Desert* (NY: New Directions, 1960) 3–24.

contradiction to the hidden life, humility, and perfect humanity of our Lord.

The fashionable idols, whether they are manifested by money, or by conspicuous consumption, or by profligate expressions of sexuality, or all of the above, are always rooted in the will to power and ego-assertion — the antithesis of the gospel of the teacher from Nazareth. In the preface to *In the Valley of Wormwood,* his collection of the lives of Cistercian saints, Merton reminds us that, '*Ama nesciri,* (love to be unknown) has always been one of the chief Cistercian ideals.'[7] We are reminded again of Philippians 2: 1-5.

I hope that monasticism's prophetic voice will always challenge idolatry and injustice. In what follows, I will briefly highlight four specifically prophetic characteristics of monasticism's 'counter-culture'.

---

[7] Thomas Merton, *In the Valley of Wormwood*, Patrick Hart, ed. (Cistercian Studies Series 233) (Collegeville, MN: Liturgical Press, 2013) xxiii.

The Prophet's 'Voice'

IF monastic life is to continue to be prophetic it must be consistent, by which I mean that a visitor to a monastery must see what is written in its Rule lived within its walls. Brilliant as Benedict's Rule is, it is useless unless lived consistently. Incongruence, disconnection between what we say and what we do, leads to stillborn witness. Let me give two non-monastic instances, two examples of inconsistency, which I have encountered recently.

The first concerns an international society that promotes spiritual direction. They encourage spiritual life and development and have done much to help people. But the monetary cost of belonging to the group is greater than that of many professional organizations, and the annual meetings are held in luxury hotels that no spiritual director whom I know could afford. When I declined an invitation to speak at their meeting and respectfully pointed out the financial inconsistency, the kind officer offered me a scholarship, completely missing the basic disconnection between the fashionable idol of affluence and the goal of deepening the spiritual life.

Secondly, I had a very pleasing assignment to give talks at a pastors' conference, on the Emmaus Road story as a template for Christian spirituality. Attending the meeting was a national officer of that church's benevolent association, the arm of the church that cares for orphans, children with serious health challenges, the elderly, widows, and so on. That person drove a luxury automobile and had an apparently large expense account with which he generously took people out for meals at nice restaurants. I should not complain; I was one of them. But I wondered about the sacrificial giving *behind* those funds, and the children and elderly for whom they were intended. I experienced a serious incongruence in the life style exhibited and the rhetoric of the agency.

I need not multiply examples. If monastic life is to be prophetic in a world that genuflects to money, power, and prestige, it must incarnate its ideals, must walk its talk. For all of us, the silence of how we live our lives speaks volumes about, and is our primary witnesses to, the actual focus of our lives, what we really believe. 'Therefore you have no excuse, whoever you are, when you judge others; for in passing judgement on another you condemn yourself, because you, the judge, are doing the very same things.' (Rom. 2: 1.) Appropriating St Paul's sleazy rhetorical trick, I remind you when you think about monastic 'poverty', please to remember that it guarantees what a lot of people in the world don't have: a safe home, clothing, food *and* both health care and reasonable assurance of care when you are old and wobbly. (When the preacher pulls a trick like this in our southern mountain churches we say that he's quit preachin' and gone to meddlin'.)

A Counter-Cultural Way of Operating

This brings me to my second, closely related point about the visibility of monasticism's prophetic voice. Monasticism is most prophetic when monastics simply live their lives unselfconsciously and consistently, because monastic life is, and always has been, counter-cultural. Monastics may still be in the world, resident in its 'kingdoms', but they are not of the world because their life refuses to clutch at its tawdry gods.

Here is an example: I once gave a talk to the Thomas Merton Society in Washington DC and stayed with the kind monks at St Anselm's Benedictine Abbey. The first evening, I went to the refectory for dinner, noting appreciatively that guests may now eat with the community. We had a meat meal, and one of monks gently leaned over and cut the serving of his elderly confrère into bite-sized pieces. I was deeply touched by this simple gesture. Where else in our society would you see two men so unselfconsciously in such a relationship? I reflected on it later to the one who had cut the meat. He looked at me as if I were from another planet and said simply, 'but he's my brother'.

'He's my brother'. That response is itself counter-cultural. Imagine a society in which the other is not enemy, stranger, competitor for scarce resources, weakling to be dominated, rival for power or sexual partner, but brother or sister. The monastic life had so formed these men that one could offer a personal, domestic service and the other could receive it. There was no whiff of power exerted or endured, no ego assertion, no enforced low self-esteem, no subtle but clear message to the elderly brother than 'old' meant 'lesser'. There was just a beautiful and memorable gesture offered and received which, in its unselfconscious ordinariness, was a vivid prophetic witness about what it really means to be a man and a monk.

Reflecting on this vivid monastic vignette led me to ask myself this question: what characteristics of ordinary monasticism might be most helpfully counter-cultural and thus prophetic, today and into the future? Four things came immediately to mind: its life of marginality; its respect for the whole of life; its life of compunction; and its concern for the other person before oneself. These are demonstrated in four key practices of traditional monasticism: hospitality, necessities according to need, manual labour, and humility.

Marginality

Marginality is clearly related to the matter of detachment. Monastic life is a prophetic witness to the importance of life on the edges, a life which Merton says in the introduction to *Wisdom of the Desert*, rejects completely 'the false, formal self, fabricated under social compulsion in "the world"'.[1] It is no coincidence that Benedictine houses developed out-lying granges, and medieval Cistercians chose remote locations for their monasteries. If monastic life is not to be co-opted by what passes for the latest wisdom or the fashionable idols of the age, monasteries and monastics must chose marginality and life at the fringes, thus practising the detachment of which I wrote earlier.

My point is not geographic; it does not mean moving all the monasteries to the desert in Utah, or to the southern Appalachian Mountains, or the Scottish Highlands or the wilds of Wales. It means a conscious, prophetic choice to distance the life itself from the accepted patterns of mainstream society. Let one example suffice. How necessary to monastic life are all the electronic gadgets that now rule (and I do mean rule) life in the world? This is a cutting-edge question for monastics. Walls used to mark boundaries that protected an appropriate remoteness in monastic life. Walls do not keep out cyberspace. How necessary to your life is constant contact by means of all manner of electronic gadgets?

---

[1] Merton, *Wisdom of the Desert*, 5.

Jesus was a marginal person. He was raised in an obscure village on the fringes of the Roman Empire — 'can anything good come out of Nazareth?' asked Nathanael (John 1: 46). He took an extreme and marginalizing view of the meaning of Torah and thought the prophets spoke God's word and wisdom. More than once I have wondered what Jesus thinks of the grand and grinding institution we call 'his Church', as if it were *his* and not what *we* have made of it. Perhaps no one has better understood this marginality, and articulated it by his life, than Charles de Foucauld who advocated the poverty and hidden-ness of Nazareth and for whom, at the turn of the twentieth century, even the Cistercians were too lax.

If your great life quest is for the latest trend, for the newest item or idea, for being at centres of power and influence, being a big player 'where it's at', may I respect-fully suggest that you're not likely to be very happy in a healthy monastery. Because, as Merton noted in connection with the desert Christians, 'the desert had no contribution to offer but a discreet and detached silence'[2].

Respect for Life

Monastic life is a lived prophetic witness to the value of life in all its manifestations, at all its stages, and in all its cycles. Esteeming and valuing life in its myriad forms is central to a Christian theology of creation. We value the living thing that is creation itself, because it came to us from the mouth of God. God spoke, and things came into being — things it is our responsibility and joy to reverence and protect. Trashing the creation is an affront to the generous generativity of God whose nature it is to make

---

[2] Ibid. 14.

and to give. To read about the development of monastic houses, and about monastic agriculture in particular, is to see ecology at work before the word was coined, or the ecological movement became as vital to the planet's survival as it is now.

Respect for life is profoundly connected, too, to a theology of the Incarnation. God chose to take on flesh, substance, the stuff of creation and, as the Eastern Church teaches, thereby divinized it. We reverence life because God gave it, assumed it, and expects to be sovereign over it. The delightful concern for the body in Benedict's Rule, (chapter 22, how to sleep; chapter 36, sick brothers; chapters 39 and 40, food and drink apportionment; chapter 55, clothing and shoes) and for the stages of life: (chapter 30, correction of youths; chapter 37, old men and children) witnesses to the seriousness with which monasticism has always taken incarnation. We remember that the gospel accounts of the risen Jesus, especially in Luke and John, stress his bodily-ness, and that the body which he took with him to heaven at the Ascension thus divinized our flesh for a second time.

Today one of the most powerful prophetic witnesses of the monastery is its treatment of its elderly members. The world warehouses the elderly, hiding them away in places where they cannot contribute to society — a living death. They can only wait for Brother Death, who is often welcomed as preferable to the zombie world of the inaccurately named 'care home'. I have visited monasteries on three continents, and have never visited one where the elder or senior monastics were not honoured and given tasks commensurate to their abilities. A Sister sits in her chair and spends the morning folding the basket of clean dishcloths. The Brother who cannot walk answers the telephone. The monastic who is ill is cared for in the infirmary, another indication that even the architectural planning of monasteries took Incarnation seriously because *sarx,* the body, and *carne,* the flesh, is impermanent by divine design. When it is time to cross the Jordan, community members pray them across. We generally understand the prophetic importance of respect for life at its outset, but can forget it is equally so at its natural diminishment and close. 'Human nature tends to show sympathy to the aged and to children', says Benedict.[3] We might pray that it will again be so in our world, and that monasteries might show the world how to do it.

Compunction

Compunction is a funny old word. We seldom hear it because it describes a psychological experience no longer much recommended lest humanity's fragile self-esteem be damaged. Compunction in its mildest form is a vague misgiving. More muscularly, it is the dis-ease caused by awareness of guilt. Compunction presumes guilt, and guilt presumes, if not moral absolutes, at least moral standards. In a world of self-gratification, no-holds-barred, and if-it-feels-good-do-it, monasticism's understanding of compunction is prophetic because it insists there are things we think or do of which we *should* be ashamed.

As is the case in respect for life, compunction incarnates an aspect of traditional and orthodox Christian theology. In the 1970's there was a school of popular psychology known as 'I'm OK–You're OK'. In response to

---

[3] *The Rule of St. Benedict* (Anthony C. Meisel & M. L. del Mastro, trans.) (NY: Doubleday/Image, 1975) 79.

this, the story of an 'eighth word' of Jesus from the cross was circulated in some theological circles. The eighth word was a question, 'If I'm OK, and you're OK, what am I doing on this cross?' Reader, I confess that I am profoundly *not* OK, and apparently, there have always been people and things in human history and society so profoundly not OK that God had to come and die to mend them. Compunction presumes the atonement, as problematic as that theological doctrine has always been.

Compunction is not scruples, straining at the gnat of any tiny mistake, developing paranoia about rules or a psychosis about correctness. Compunction is an aid to growth in holiness. Its healthy recognition of our imperfections and our besetting sins assists our spiritual growth because recognition is the first step toward amendment. Compunction accounts for classic monastic teachings, like those of Evagrius or John Climacus or Cassian, and recent works like Meg Funk's *Thoughts Matter* or Lawrence Cunningham's *The Seven Deadly Sins: A Visitor's Guide*[4]. Maria Boulding was particularly good at helping us understand the difference between humanness and actual faults or sins: she wrote, 'We do not need to apologize to [God] for being human.'[5]

Along with humility, compunction is fundamental to monastic formation. Thomas Merton taught that it linked sorrow and joy. The meaning of compunction is 'a sorrow

---

[4] Lawrence S. Cunningham, *The Seven Deadly Sins: A Visitor's Guide* (Notre Dame, IN: Ave Maria Press, 2012); Mary Margaret Funk, *Thoughts Matter* (NY: Continuum, 2004); Angela Tilby, *The Seven Deadly Sins* (London: SPCK, 2009).

[5] Maria Boulding OSB, *Gateway to Resurrection* (London: Burns & Oats, 2010) 36.

which pierces, which liberates, which gives hope and therefore joy'.

> Such sorrow brings joy because it is … the acceptance of one's actual condition, and the acceptance of reality is always a liberation from the burden of illusion which we strive to justify by our errors and sins. Compunction is a necessary sorry, but it is followed by joy and relief because it wins for us one of the greatest blessings, the light of truth and the grace of humility.[6]

Leclercq also makes explicit this connection between compunction and spiritual growth. He explains that the word was originally a medical term describing an attack of acute pain:

> Compunction becomes a pain of the spirit … resulting from two causes: the existence of sin and our own tendency toward sin … and the existence of our desire for God and even our very possession of God.

It is

> an act of God in us … by which God awakens us …. Compunction hollows us and thereby increases our capacity for God.[7]

Other-directedness

Because compunction often arises in connection with our mistakes in relationship, it leads to the fourth counter-cultural or prophetic witness of monasticism, what I call 'other-directedness'. St Paul taught that every charism

---

[6] Thomas Merton, *Seasons of Celebration* (New York: Farrar, Straus & Giroux, 1965) 115–116.
[7] Leclercq, 37–39.

God gives to individuals in the Church is for the sake of the whole Church (cf. Rom. 12: 1-8; I Cor. 12: 1-12; Eph. 4: 11-13). Thus, a monastic vocation is not only for the person who has received it, but also for the whole Church, indeed, for the whole creation. The life of the monastic reflects that of the Lord Jesus in his *kenotic* orientation: he emptied himself (Phil. 2: 6-11), poured himself out, like the anointing woman's precious nard (Mark 14: 3-9). Monastic life is a life of self-giving in imitation of the Christ who came not to be served but to serve and give his life. Maria Boulding puts it beautifully: 'God always gives before he asks, and he gives us life before asking us to give our lives away. His Trinitarian life is infinite giving.'[8]

Western society generally, and the American ethos in particular, operates according to the myth of the rugged, self-sufficient individual. This, of course, is a total fiction, but one so pervasive as to be formative in the lives of many people. On the other hand, the prophetic witness of monasticism is expressed along the lines of 'we all get there or none of us get there'. I am sure you have heard about the Desert Elder who had finished his baskets, put the handles on them and was ready to go to market when he heard a brother say that the market was about to begin, and he had nothing to make handles for his baskets. Whereupon the elder took the handles off his own baskets and gave them to the younger monk. And the punch line is: 'Thus in his great charity he saw to it that his brother's work was finished while his own

---

[8] Boulding, 30.

remained incomplete.'[9] Other-directedness can set aside its own goals to forward those of others.

In a world of striving for individual success and ego gratification, a community which embodies such other-directedness is radically prophetic in ways which I hope will always apply. Monasteries have always practiced *koinonia*, sharing in a common life. *Koinos* in Greek means common, hence 'common-ness', fellowship and participation, communion and sharing. Four practices in particular demonstrate the other-directedness of the monastic life: hospitality, necessities supplied according to need, manual labour and humility.

1. *Hospitality*: Chapter 53 of the Rule of St Benedict, concerning the reception of guests, begins with a gospel reference that can be applied more generally to practices of other-directedness: 'All guests to the monastery should be welcomed as Christ, because He will say, "I was a stranger, and you took me in" (Matt. 25: 35).'[10] Hospitality offered to the stranger has always characterized monasteries, but guests need not have access to the whole household, and, while open to guests, monasteries, like families, can still maintain appropriate boundaries.

The hospitality of the house must be extended to hospitality of the heart, the welcome of the stranger in the guise not only of other people and cultures, but also of other ideas and ways of seeing reality. In 'A Letter to Pablo Antonio Cuadra Concerning Giants', Thomas Merton provided the theological rationale for such hospitality: 'Since the Word became flesh, God is in man. God is in *all men*. All men are to be seen and treated as

---

[9] As related in Merton, *Wisdom of the Desert*, 71.
[10] Rule of St Benedict (RB) 89.

Christ.'[11] Merton continues, 'God speaks, and God is to be heard, not only on Sinai, not only in my own heart, but in the *voice of the stranger*. We must find him in our enemy, or we may lose him even in our friend.'[12]

2.   *Providing for others according to their need*: The principle here is that I consume no more resources than I need, so that my sisters and brothers will have what they need. If that principle and practice is not radically prophetic in the current environment, I do not know what is. It certainly describes a better economic system than capitalism, and a more Christian one. The current extraordinary and unjust income disparity between the rich and the poor suggests a lot of us did not learn the basic kindergarten lesson of sharing. In the discussion about the community of goods in *The Cistercian Way*, Andre Louf points out that the desire to possess is an attempt to fill the void that keeps us open to the experience of God. To share possessions is to be open to the good of the brethren as well as to be poor in the sense of needing others.[13] Both ideas are very much to the point in a consideration of other-directedness.

3.   *Manual labour*: The same simple ideal of sharing, of *koinonia*, undergirds monastic manual labour, the work (*labora*) which is for the sake of prayer (*ora*). Cassian taught that work was the anchor that stabilizes the heart.[14] We work not only to support the life of prayer, but also to support our sisters or brothers. To do so, as Charles de Foucauld so clearly articulated, is to share the life of that

---

[11] Merton, *The Complete Poems*, 380.

[12] Ibid. 384.

[13] Andre Louf, *The Cistercian Way* (Kalamazoo: Cistercian Publications, 1989) 90-91.

[14] Ibid. 116.

humble working man, Jesus of Nazareth. Dom Louf points out that 'Real work by which we truly earn our bread is a feature of poverty.'[15] Not to work is to fall victim to idleness, which Benedict calls 'the enemy of the soul'. 'They are truly monks', he says, 'when they must live by manual labour.'[16]

All those hundreds of years ago, Benedict suggested something like the eight-hour workday that only became law in the twentieth century. Earlier we considered work in the context of holy leisure (*otium*). To over-do *labora*, to make the monastery a factory, is to miss the point of work and to destroy its prophetic witness. It may also destroy a fellow monk, for of labour Benedict says, 'Everything should be in moderation ... for the sake of the timorous'.[17]

4. *Humility*: The prophetic witness of monasticism's other-directedness is seen most clearly in the practiced virtue of humility.[18] St Bernard said, 'Unless the spiritual edifice is built on the foundation of humility, it will most certainly collapse.'[19] One dare not argue the point. Benedict opens chapter 7, devoted to the rungs of the ladder of humility, with the words of Jesus, 'Everyone who exalts himself shall be humbled, and he who humbles himself shall be exalted' (Luke 14: 11). In the world in which we live, nothing is more prophetic than a life lived in humility. And until the Parousia, the end of

---

[15] Ibid. 115.

[16] RB 86.

[17] Ibid.

[18] I highly recommend Andre Louf's little book, *The Way of Humility*, trans. Lawrence S. Cunningham, (Monastic Wisdom Series, 11) (Kalamazoo, MI: Cistercian Publications, 2007).

[19] Quoted in Leon Cristiani, *St. Bernard of Clairvaux*, trans. M. Angeline Bouchard, (Boston: Daughters of St. Paul, 1983) 150.

time, I suspect this will always be true. Along with love, it is the enduring virtue and the one which characterized our Lord Jesus, who said of himself, 'I am gentle and humble of heart'. (Matt. 11: 29). Living life gently and humbly will always be profoundly prophetic as it stands between, and links, the perfection of God and the aspirations of the human heart.

Conclusion

Most of us know that there are both benevolent forces in the spiritual life, and there are malevolent ones. Monastic life exists, and will continue to exist, to right spiritual balances. We live, and I suspect humans have always lived, in a time of great darkness and evil. A life oriented toward God alone provides an enlightening counter-balance to the darkness. It is not only a light *in* darkness, but it actively helps to keep the darkness at bay, even, and especially when, we cannot see how this is so.

Monasticism's way forward is to remain rooted in the traditional basic 'h's' of monastic life: humility, holiness, hospitality, human-ness and humour. To contradict easy accommodation to the fashionable idols of the age, monastics live the vows, which, as Thomas Merton noted in his first talk and introduction to the life of the vows, 'enable us to *be* someone, not to do something'. Merton continues:

> What God seeks of us is *His own image in ourselves.* Our job in life is not so much to produce anything, as *to be what we are supposed to be,* to let the divine image come out and manifest itself in our lives by the *way in which we live.*[20]

---

[20] Merton, *The Life of the Vows*, 9. Merton's italics.

I give (almost) the last word to John of Fécamp, an eleventh-century Benedictine abbot in Normandy whose writings were the most widely read spiritual texts before *The Imitation of Christ*. As his long prose poem 'The City of God,' which is also a prayer, draws to a close he writes:

> Let us be happy because of what has already been accomplished in the faithful who, yesterday, were fighting for Christ, and today reign with Him in glory. Let us be happy because of what has been told us in truth: We shall go to the land of the living.[21]

It is my prayer that monasticism will always incarnate God's truth and be an outpost of the eternal land of the living in a world that is passing away.

---

[21] Quoted in Leclercq, 82–83.